MY STORY · MY LIFE

A Journal of Self-Discovery

Nancy Hoffman, PsyD

Bella Vida Press

My Story, My Life
Copyright © 2012 Nancy Hoffman, PsyD

Published by Bella Vida Press
PO Box 342
Corte Madera, California 94976
www.bellavidapress.com

For contact information or to order books, see www.bellavidapress.com

ISBN: 978-0-9795947-0-0

Design & Composition: Christi Payne, Page & Book, Astoria, Oregon
Printed by Lightning Source, Inc. in the United States

The greatest gift we can give the people in our lives is the gift of ourselves. *My Story, My Life* is a journal that is ultimately meant to be shared with family, friends, and loved ones.

Since the structure of every life is different, not all of the pages in this journal will be relevant to you. This is a record of your journey and it should reflect the unique story of your life as much as possible. This book is merely a tool intended to get you started on the road of reflection.

Every life has value, beauty, and meaning. It is my hope that, by reflecting on your journey, on the story of your life, you will come to understand and honor the contribution that you make to the world.

As Irish poet Galway Kinnell writes:

> Everything flowers from within of self-blessing;
> though sometimes it is necessary
> to re-teach a thing its loveliness . . .

Here's to your loveliness!

My Story, My Life
by

_____

_____

I dedicate this book to

. . . .

With love from

. . . .

In the year

. . . .

Oh that my words were written!
Oh that they were inscribed in a book!

JOB 19:23

In the Beginning

My given name is

I was named for

Nicknames

Date of birth

Place of birth

Weight   Length

Hair color   Eyes

My Godparents

The accent of one's birthplace lingers in the mind
and in the heart as it does in one's speech.

Duc De La Rochefoucauld

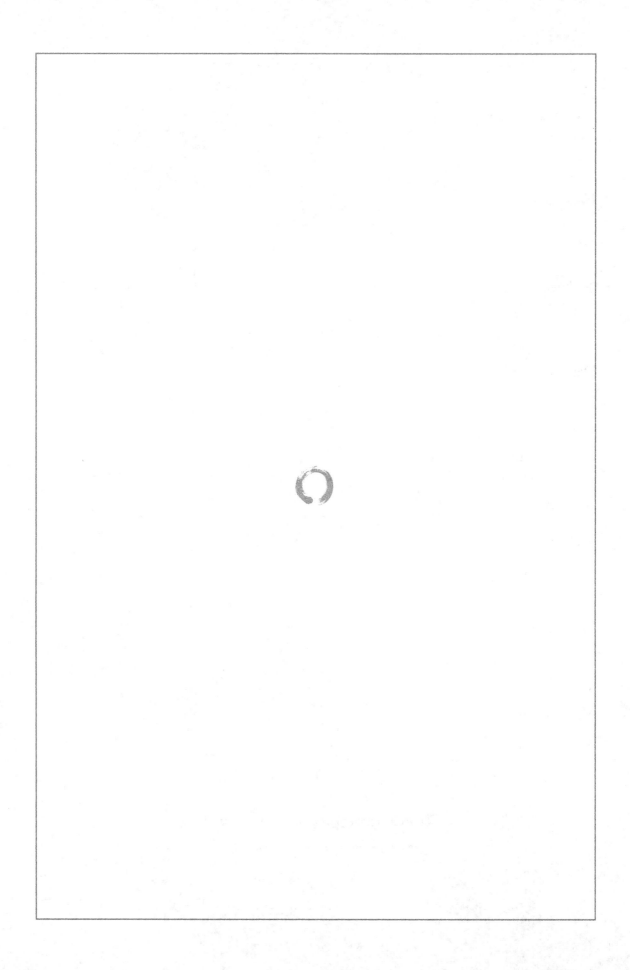

My Family Tree

My mother   Birth date   Birth place

_____

Her parents   Birth date   Birth place

_____

_____

Her grandparents   Birth date   Birth place

_____

_____

_____

_____

My father   Birth date   Birth place

_____

His parents   Birth date   Birth place

_____

_____

His grandparents   Birth date   Birth place

_____

_____

_____

_____

My ancestors came from   in the year

_____

_____

_____

_____

The initial mystery that attends any journey is:
How did the traveller reach his starting point in the first place?

LOUISE BOGAN

Family History

The origin of our family name

The first members of our family to settle in this country

Where they settled and why

People will not look forward to posterity,
who never look backward to their ancestors.

EDMUND BURKE

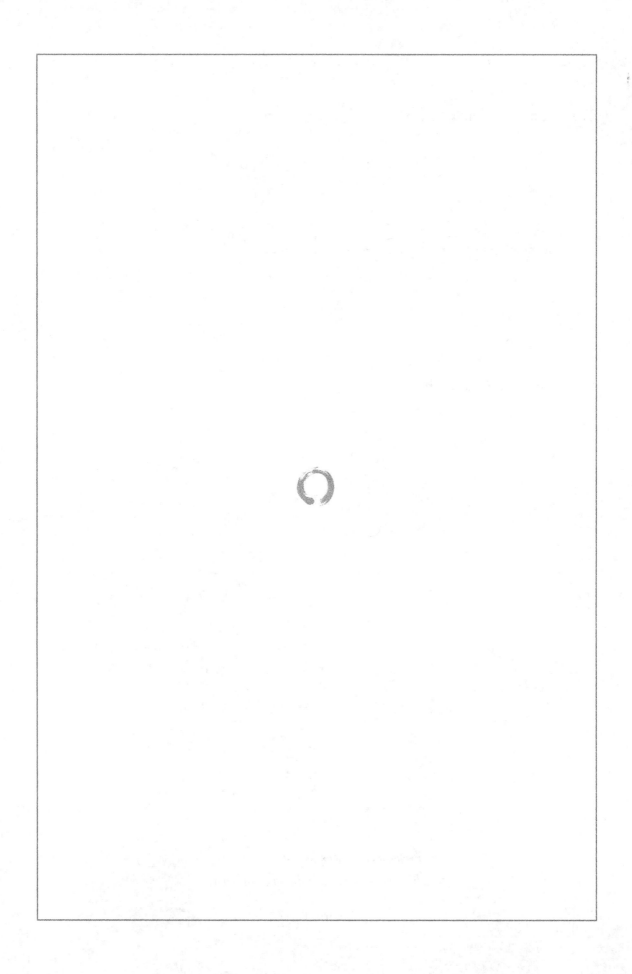

Family History

Stories I've heard about my ancestors

How they earned their living

Hardships they endured

To forget one's ancestors is to be a brook without a source,
a tree without a root.

CHINESE PROVERB

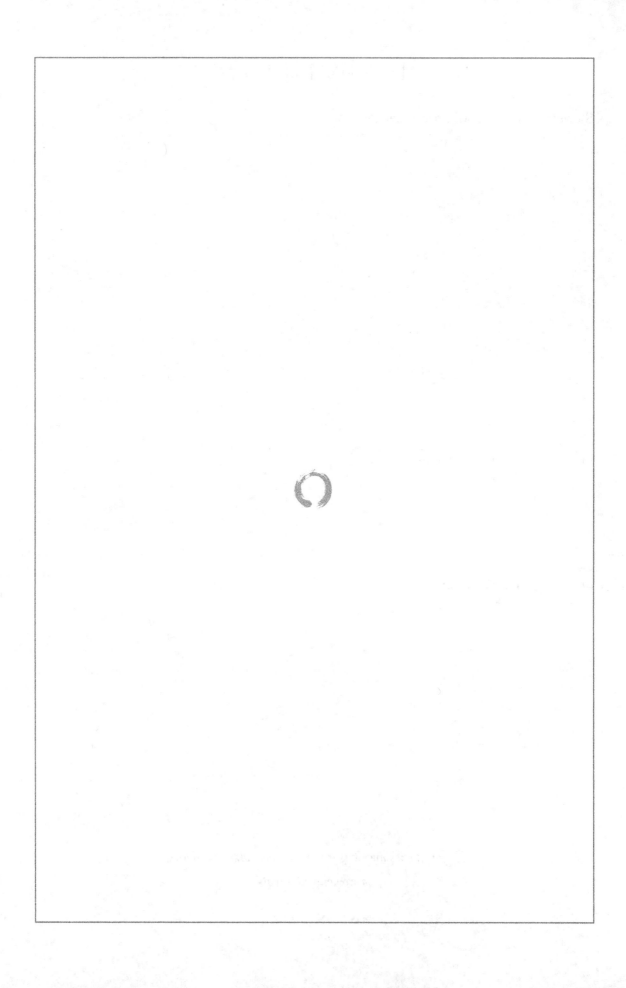

Family Traditions

My favorite holiday

What it means to me

It is of great importance that the need for creating unity is recognized.
The human spirit is nourished by a sense of connectedness.

I CHING No. 8

Family Traditions

How we celebrate

Other holidays we celebrate

Life must be understood backwards.

Soren Kierkegaard

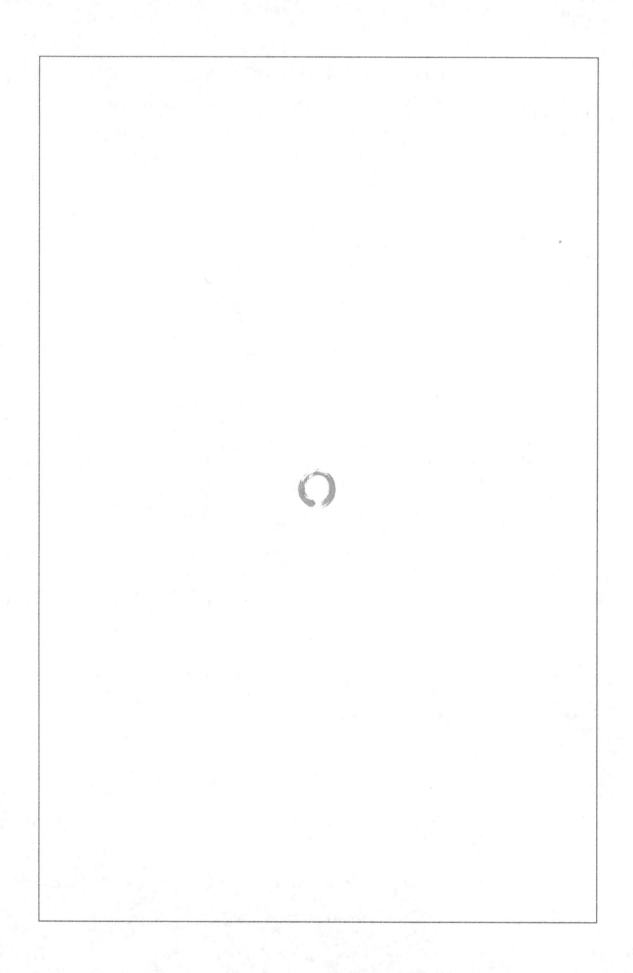

Family Recipe for a Special Event

This recipe was given to me by

My memory of eating this

Gastronomy is and always has been connected with its sister art of love.

M.F.K. FISHER

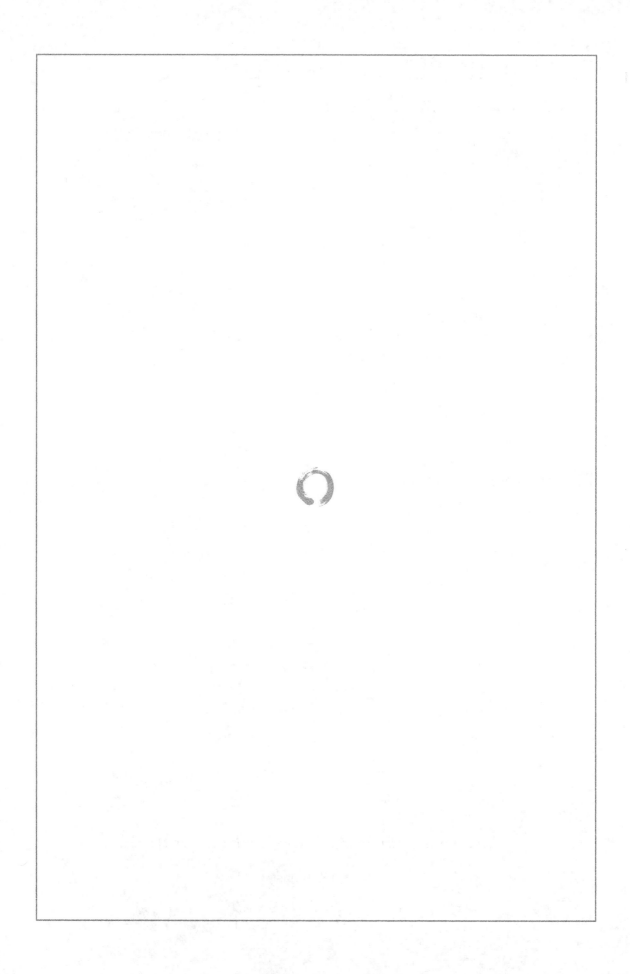

Family Recipe for a Special Event

This recipe was given to me by

My memory of eating this

Tell me what you eat and I will tell you what you are.

ANTHELME BRILLAT-SAVARIN

Family Recipe for a Special Event

This recipe was given to me by

My memory of eating this

*Reach into your memory and look for what has restored you, what helps you recover
from the sheer hellishness of life, what food actually regenerates your system, not so
you can leap tall buildings but so you can turn off the alarm clock with vigor.*

JIM HARRISON

My Mother

My mother's name

What I called her

Height   Weight   Hair   Eyes

How she looked to me

Her vocation

What I admired about her

My favorite memory of her

Beginning as one loving whole, a single world, mother and child will in time become separate beings;
just as lovers, beginning as two separate beings, in time become one world, one whole.

Diane Ackerman

My Father

My father's name

What I called him

Height   Weight   Hair   Eyes

How he looked to me

His vocation

What I admired about him

My favorite memory of him

*My father was very sure about certain matters pertaining to the universe.
To him, all good things—trout as well as eternal salvation—come by grace
and grace comes by art and art does not come easy.*

NORMAN MACLEAN

My Parents

How they met

Their wedding date

Where they were married

My favorite memory of them together

What I learned from them

No sooner met, but they looked; no sooner looked but they loved;
no sooner loved but they sighed; no sooner sighed but they asked one another the reason;
no sooner knew the reason but they sought the remedy:
and in these degrees have they made a pair of stairs to marriage. . .

WILLIAM SHAKESPEARE

My Maternal Grandparents

My grandmother   My grandfather

How they met

Their wedding date   Where they were married

My favorite memory of them together

What I learned from them

God bless the roots! Body and soul are one.

Theodore Roethke

My Paternal Grandparents

My grandmother

My grandfather

How they met

Their wedding date

Where they were married

My favorite memory of them together

What I learned from them

If the only prayer you say in your whole life is "Thank you," that would suffice.

MEISTER ECKHART

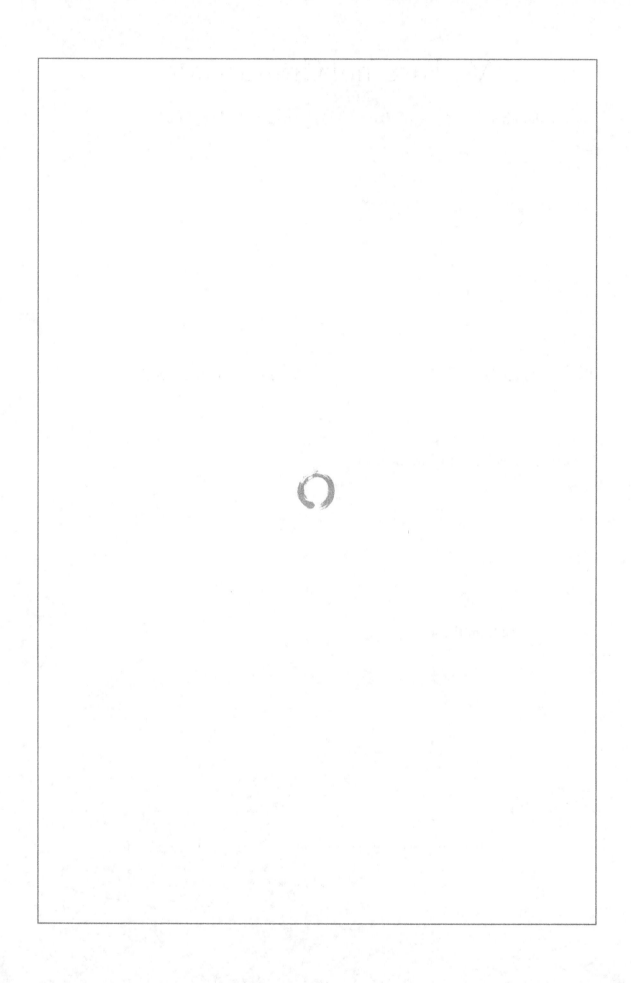

My Brothers & Sisters

Name   Birth date   Birth place

My favorite memories of them

Things we used to do

A funny family story

For one human being to love another is perhaps the most difficult task of all, the epitome, the ultimate test.
It is that striving for which all other striving is merely preparation.

Rainer Maria Rilke

The Rest of the Family

My favorite relatives

My cousins

Things we used to do

The black sheep of our family

A funny family story

 *Fate chooses your relations, you choose your friends.*

JACQUES DELILLE

When I Was Young

Where I lived

From   to

Where I went to school

What I remember most is

Where I lived

From   to

Where I went to school

What I remember most is

In my beginning is my end.

T.S. ELIOT

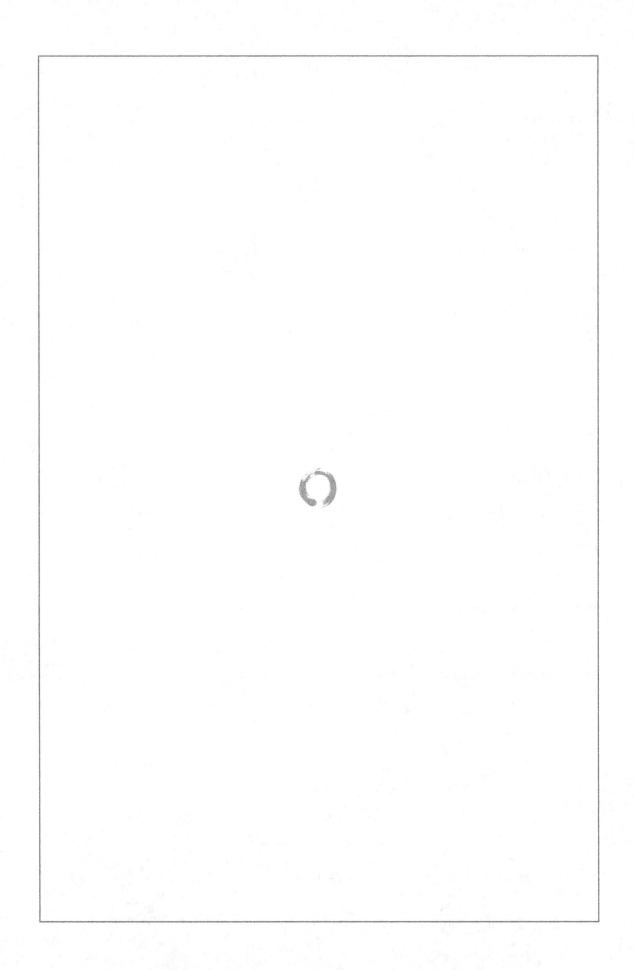

When I Was Young

Where I lived

From   to

Where I went to school

What I remember most is

Where I lived

From   to

Where I went to school

What I remember most is

God created man because He loves a good story.

ELIE WIESEL

Where I Live Now

My home now

How I got here

*The advantage of living is not measured by
length, but by use; some men have lived long,
and lived little; attend to it while you are in it.*

MICHEL EYQUEM DE MONTAIGNE

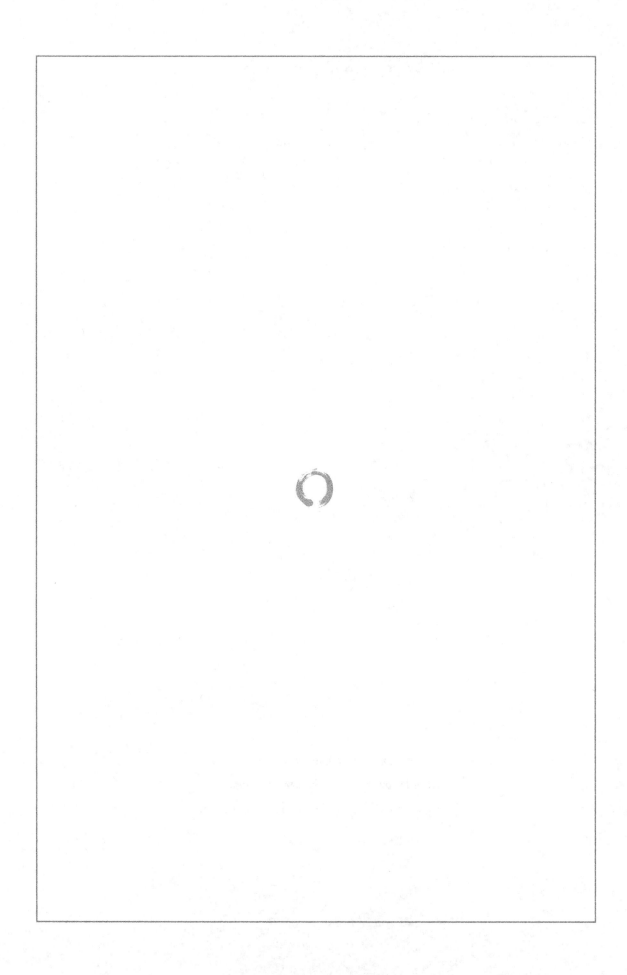

My Earliest Memories

I wake to sleep, and take my waking slow.
I feel my fate in what I cannot fear.
I learn by going where I have to go.

THEODORE ROETHKE

My Favorite Memories

The house where I grew up

My bedroom

Favorite hiding places

My chores

Family pets

What I liked to do

Oft, in the stilly night, / Eve slumber's chain has bound me
Fond memory brings the light / of other days around me.

THOMAS MOORE

My Favorite Memories

Favorite games

My favorite childhood book

My favorite toys

My favorite friend

What I wanted to be when I grew up

My first love

*Somehow I had to send myself back, with words as catalysts,
to open the memories out and see what they had to offer.*

ROY BRADBURY

The World I Lived In

Popular music and dances

My favorite songs

Newsmakers

The price of things (milk, eggs, bread, stamps, gas . . .)

Talent develops in quiet places,
character in the full current of human life.

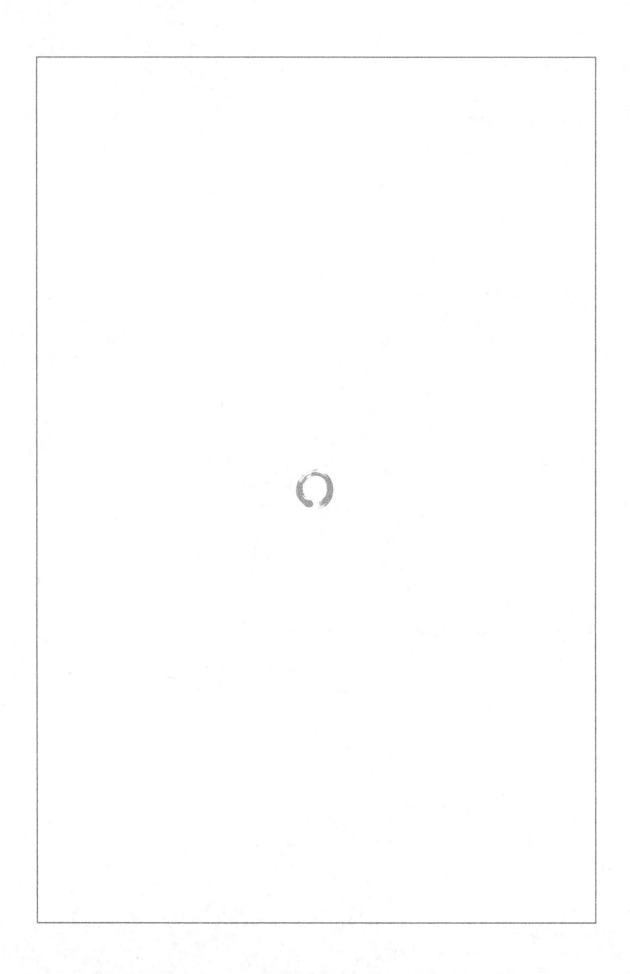

The World I Lived In

Fashions and fads

Inventions I've seen and how they've changed my life

The things I remember most

Time is like a river made up of the events which happen, and its current is strong:
no sooner does everything appear than it is swept away, and another
comes in its place, and will be swept away too.

MARCUS AURELIUS

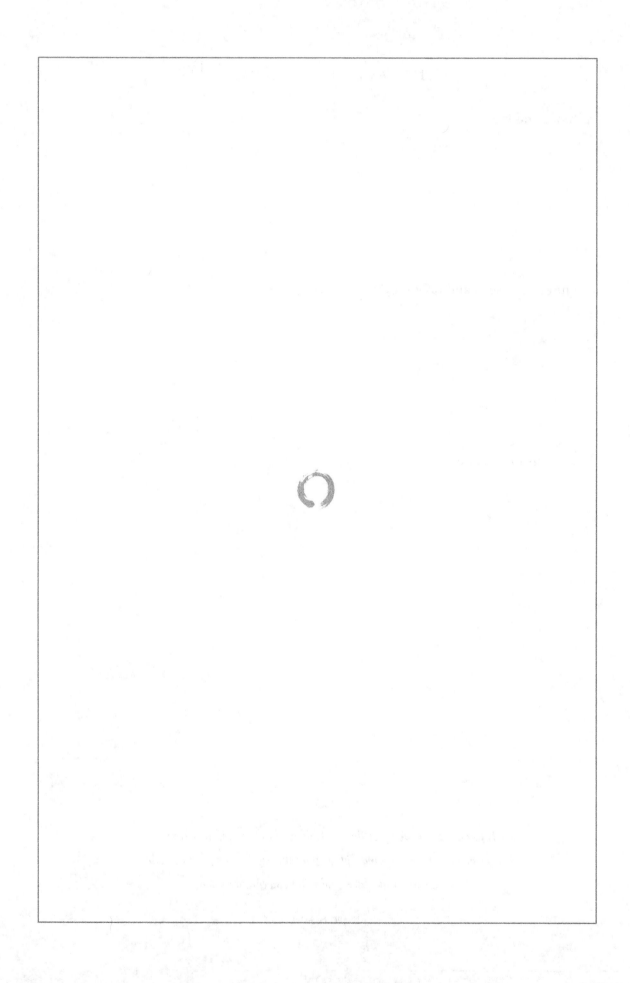

What Influenced Me

Who has had the most influence on me and why

Books that have influenced me

Teachers that have influenced me

Causes that I have worked for

Let yourself be silently drawn
by the stronger pull of what you really love.

RUMI

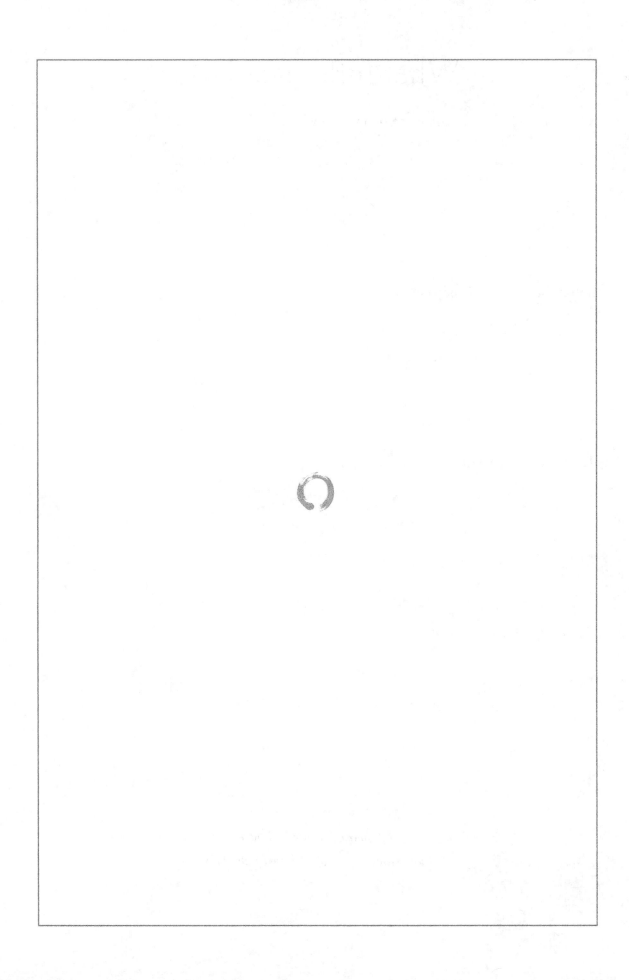

My Gifts to the World

My greatest accomplishment

Because

If I could I would change

Something I've always wanted to do

*"Goodbye," said the fox. "And now here is my secret,
a very simple secret: It is only with the heart that one
can see rightly; what is essential is invisible to the eye."*

ANTOINE DE SAINT-EXUPERY

My True Love

Name

How we met

My first impression

Our first date

Our relationship

Someday, after we have mastered the winds, the waves, the tides and gravity,
we shall harness the energies of love.
Then, for the second time in the history of the world,
we will have discovered fire.

PIERRE TEILHARD DE CHARDIN

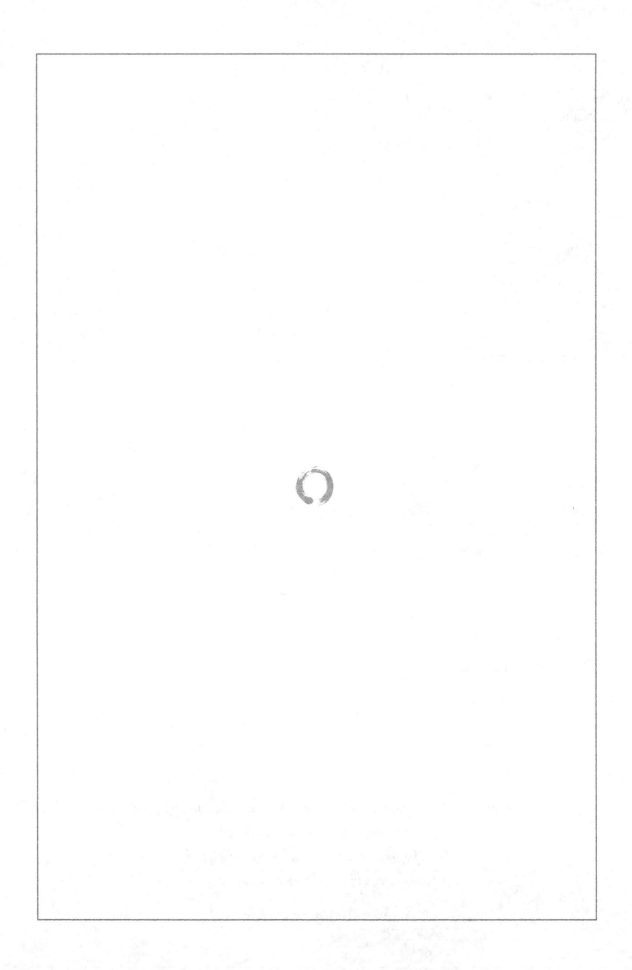

Other Loves

My thoughts on love

Each time of life has its own kind of love.

LEO TOLSTOY

My First Child

Name   Nickname

Birth date   Birth place

Weight   Height   Hair   Eyes

On the day you were born

Favorite memories

Home is where one starts from.

T.S. ELIOT

My Second Child

Name

Nickname

Birth date

Birth place

Weight   Height   Hair   Eyes

On the day you were born

Favorite memories

Not knowing when the dawn will come
I open every door.

EMILY DICKINSON

My Third Child

Name

Nickname

Birth date

Birth place

Weight   Height   Hair   Eyes

On the day you were born

Favorite memories

From wonder into wonder. Existence opens.

LAO-TSU

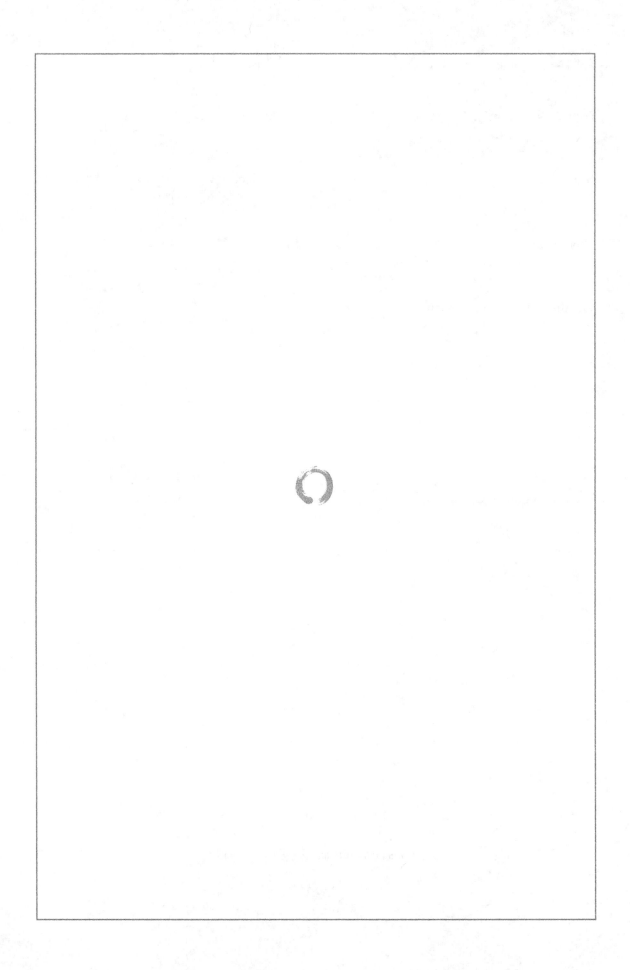

My Fourth Child

Name

Nickname

Birth date

Birth place

Weight   Height

Hair   Eyes

On the day you were born

Favorite memories

We all live under the same sky, but we don't all have the same horizon.

KONRAD ADENAUER

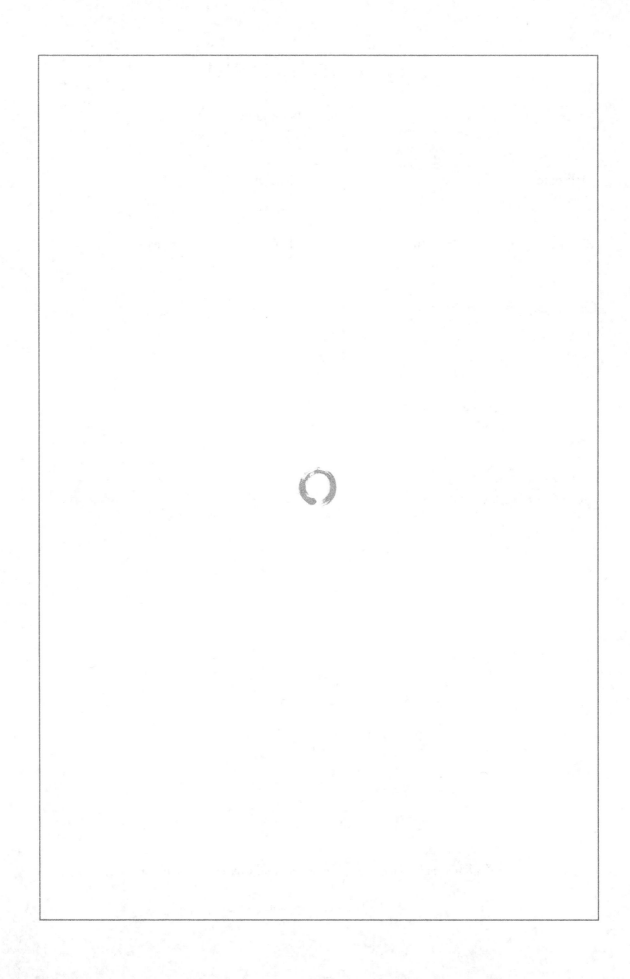

Other Children

Nobody, not even poets, has ever measured how much the heart can hold.

ZELDA FITZGERALD

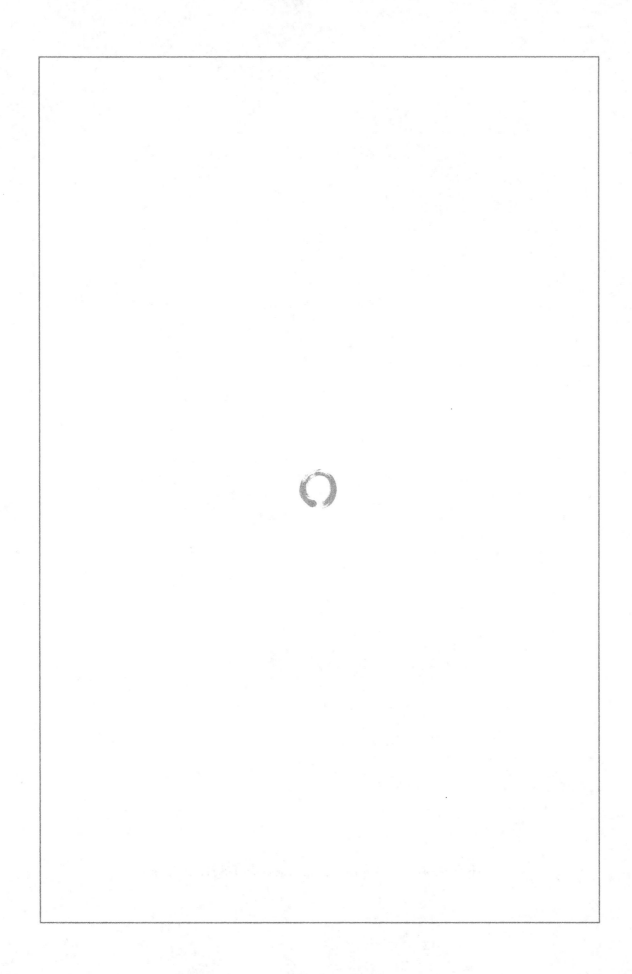

My Friends

Name

_____

How we met

_____

Memories I'll cherish

_____

_____

_____

_____

_____

_____

Name

_____

How we met

_____

Memories I'll cherish

_____

_____

_____

_____

_____

Friends are God's apology for relations.

HUGH KINGSMILL

My Friends

Name

How we met

Memories I'll cherish

Name

How we met

Memories I'll cherish

Friendship is a long conversation.
I suppose I could imagine a nonverbal friendship
revolving around shared physical work or sport,
but for me, good talk is the point of the thing.

<small>PHILLIP LOPATE</small>

My Friends

Name

How we met

Memories I'll cherish

Name

How we met

Memories I'll cherish

The meeting of two personalities is like the contact of two chemical substances:
If there is any reaction, both are transformed.

C.G. JUNG

My Professional Life

My profession

Where I went to school

Why I chose this profession

What I like most about it

What I dislike about it

*Everyone has been made for some particular work and the desire
for that work has been put in his heart.*

RUMI

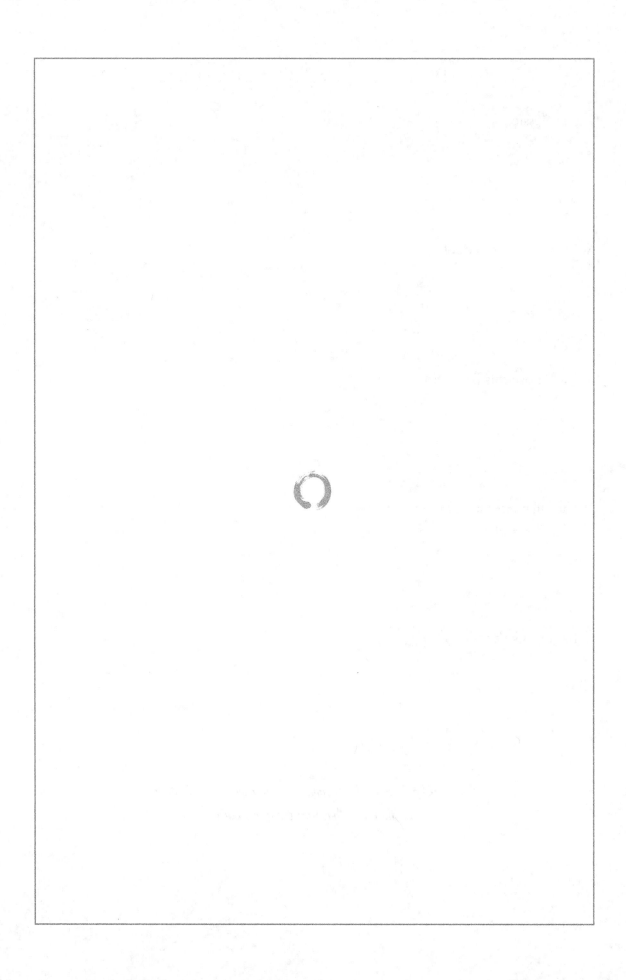

My Professional Life

Professional accomplishments I'm proud of

If I had to do it over again

Blessed is he who has found his work.
Let him ask no other blessing.

THOMAS CARLYLE

My Spiritual Life

My religion

I believe

What this means to me

Thence we came to see the stars again.

DANTE

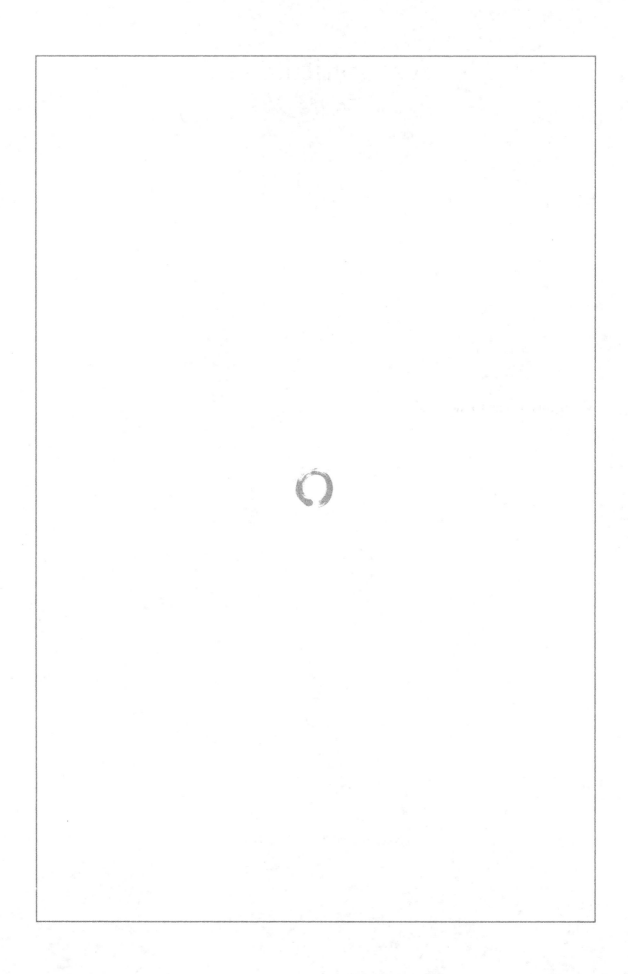

The Difficult Times

The most difficult time in my life

How it changed me

What I've learned from it

I have been acquainted with the night.

Robert Frost

The Difficult Times

Another difficult time in my life

How it changed me

What I've learned from it

The wound is the place where the light enters you.

RUMI

Mirror, Mirror on the Wall

What I like about myself and my life

What I'd like to change

Only the mediocre man is always at his best.

W. Somerset Maugham

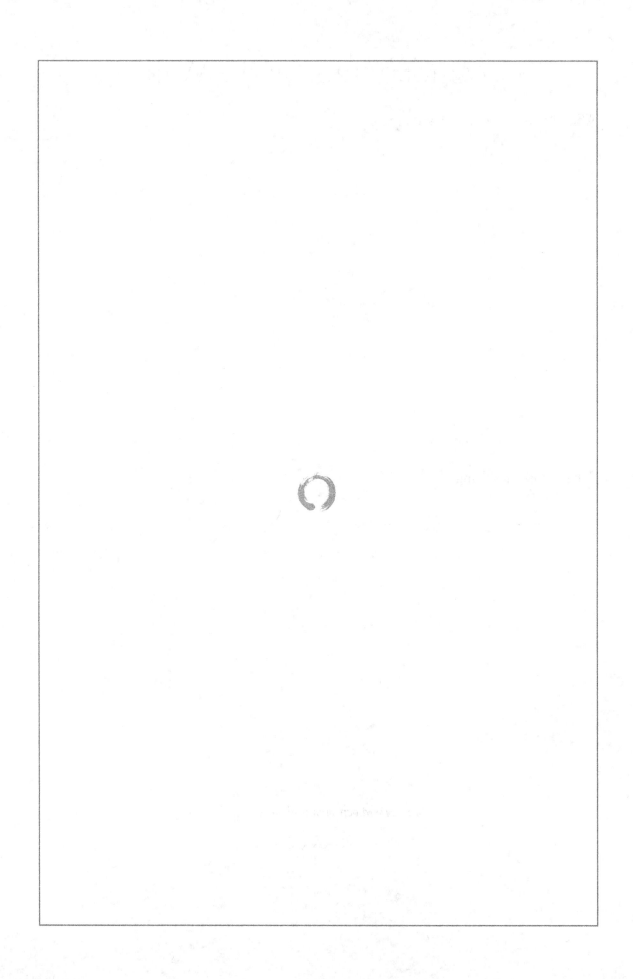

Hopes & Dreams

Yes: I am a dreamer. For a dreamer is one who can
find his way by moonlight, and see the dawn
before the rest of the world.

OSCAR WILDE

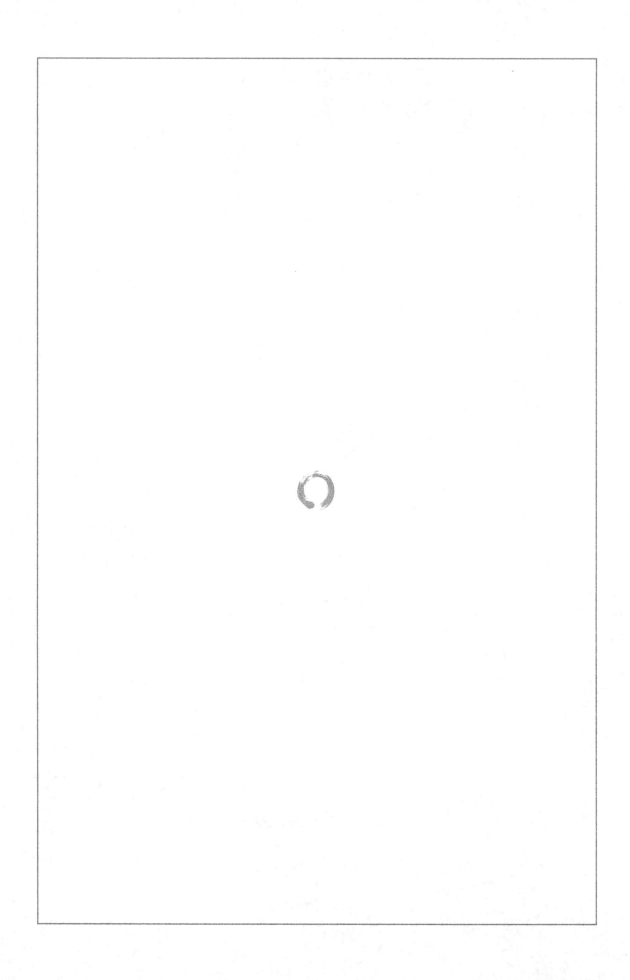

What Makes Me Happy

It took me a lifetime to learn that happiness is in quiet things, not the peaks of ecstasy.

My Favorite Possessions
(And why they're important to me)

 What if we took more seriously this capacity of things to be close to us, to reveal their beauty and expressive subjectivity? The result would be a soul-ecology, a responsibility to the things of the world based on appreciation and relatedness rather than on abstract principle.

THOMAS MOORE

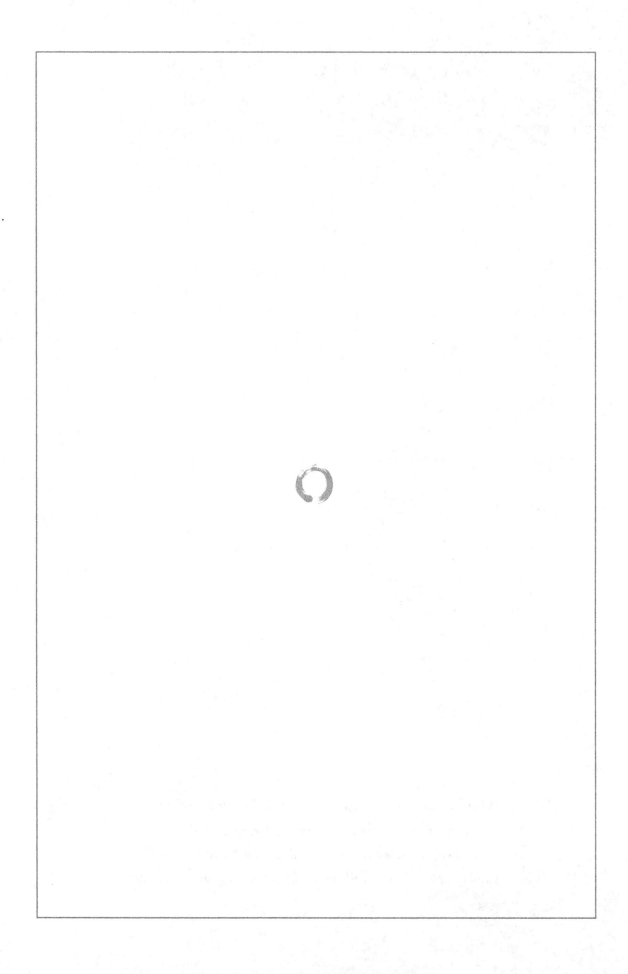

The Road Not Taken

How I thought my life would be different

Regrets

Footfalls echo in the memory
Down the passage which we did not take.

T.S. ELIOT

Before I Die

Things I'd like to do

"You have been my friend," replied Charlotte. "That in itself is a tremendous thing.
I wove my webs for you because I liked you. After all, what's a life anyway?
We're born, we live a little while, we die. A spider's life can't help being something
of a mess, with all this trapping and eating flies. By helping you, perhaps
I was trying to lift up my life a trifle. Heaven
knows anyone's life can stand a little of that."

E.B. WHITE, *Charlotte's Web*

What I've Learned About Life

Express yourself completely, and then keep quiet.

Tao Te Ching

How Others See Me
(To be written by family and friends)

*The master gives himself up to
whatever the moment brings.*

TAO TE CHING

How Others See Me

(To be written by family and friends)

There is only one thing in the world
 *worse than being talked about,*
and that is not being talked about.

OSCAR WILDE

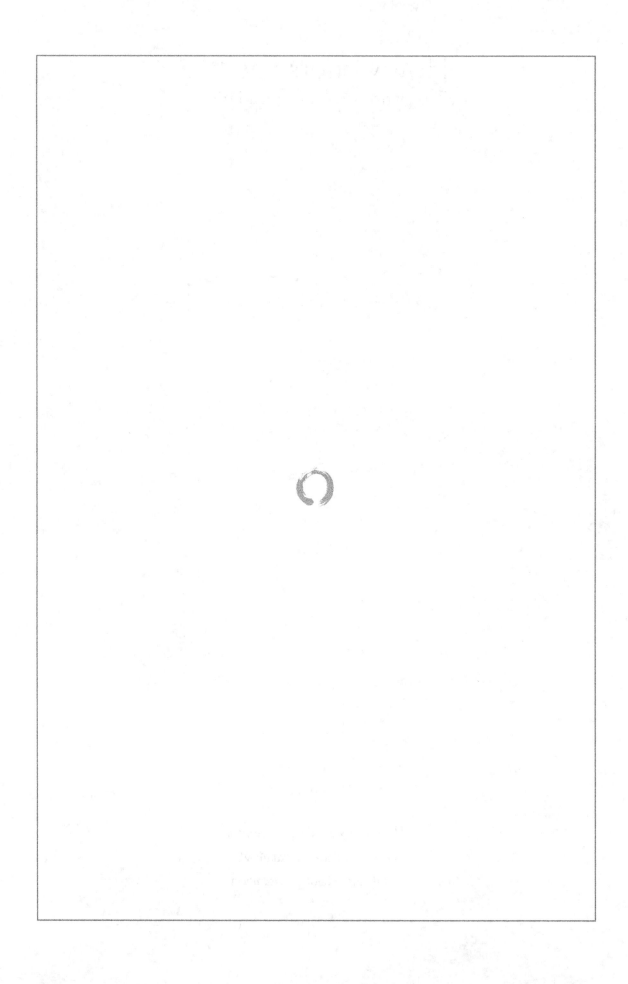

How I'd Like to Be Remembered

Although to be driven back upon oneself is an uneasy affair at best, rather like trying to cross a border with borrowed credentials, it seems to me now the one condition necessary to the beginnings of real self-respect.

JOAN DIDION

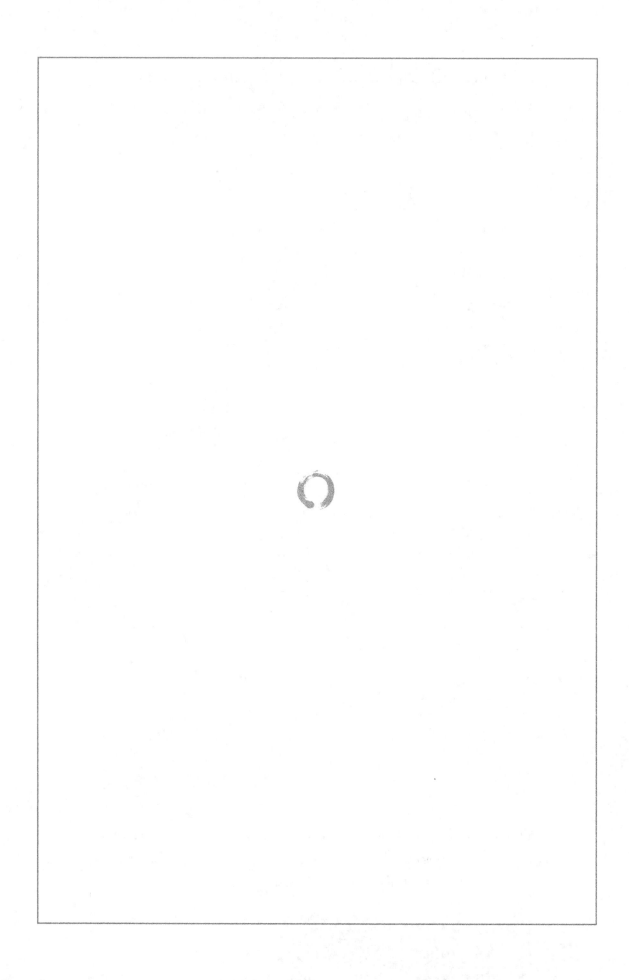

My Life

If I could take one memory with me into the afterlife, what would it be, and why?

It is not the answer that enlightens, but the question.

EUGENE IONESCO

Memories I'd Like to Share

On an occasion of this kind it becomes more than a moral
duty to speak one's mind. It becomes a pleasure.

<small>OSCAR WILDE</small>

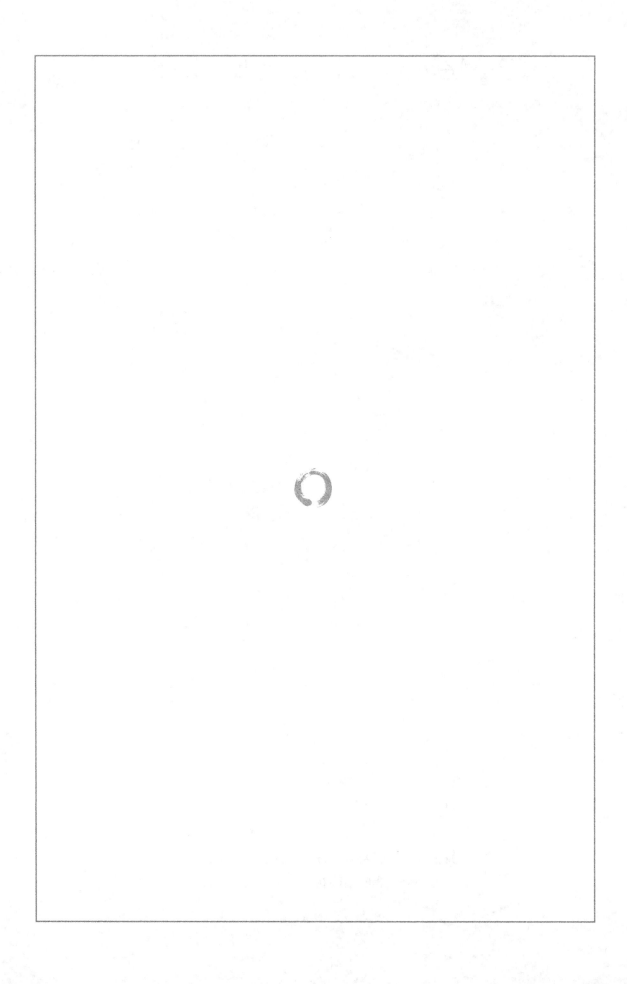

Memories I'd Like to Share

Now is not the time to think of what you do not have.
Think of what you can do with what there is.

ERNEST HEMINGWAY

And Always Remember…

What a wonderful life I've had!
I only wish I'd realized it sooner.

COLETTE

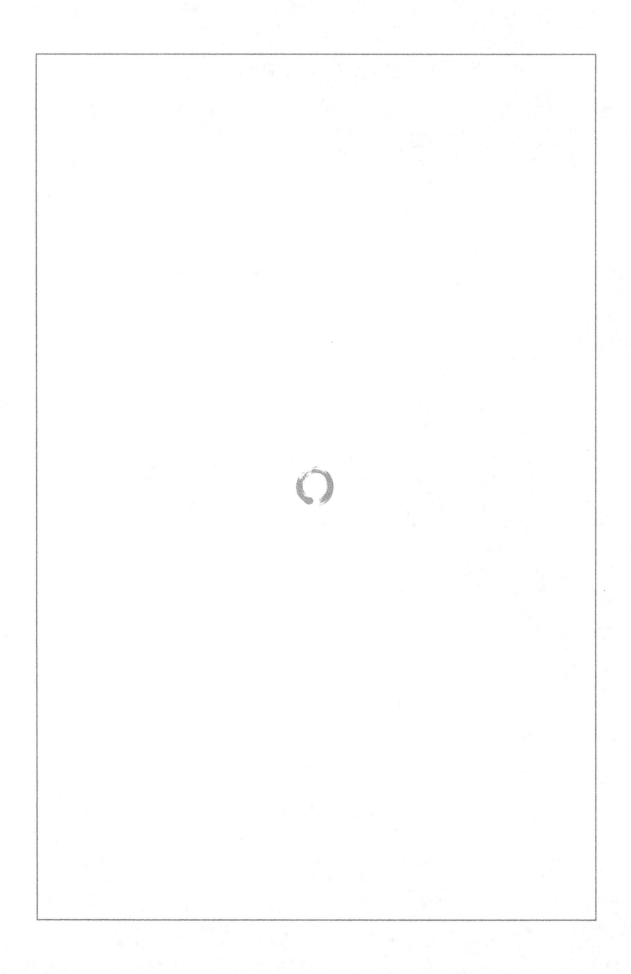

Be patient toward all that is unsolved in your heart,
and try to love the questions themselves.

RAINER MARIA RILKE

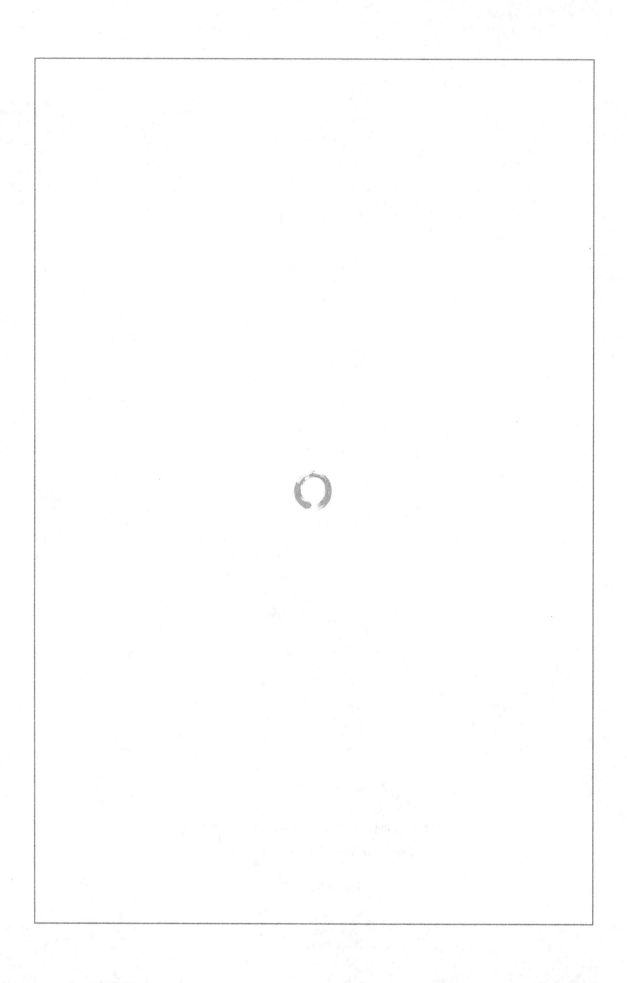

Life is what we make it.
Always has been, always will be.

Grandma Moses

CPSIA information can be obtained
at www.ICGtesting.com
Printed in the USA
LVHW102128181120
672119LV00003B/4